CALL MR. ROBESON
A life, with songs.

A Monodrama

by

TAYỌ ALUKO

Published by Playdead Press 2013

© Tayọ Aluko 2013

Tayọ Aluko has asserted his rights under the
Copyright, Design and Patents Act, 1988, to be
identified as the author of this work.

A CIP catalogue record for this book is available from
the British Library.

ISBN 978-0-9576792-5-2

Printed by BPUK

Playdead Press
www.playdeadpress.com

Call Mr. Robeson was premiered at the Edinburgh Festival Fringe on August 12th 2007 with Tayọ Aluko as Paul Robeson and Michael Conliffe as Lawrence Brown.

Other notable performances include its African premiere at the Agip Hall at MUSON, Lagos, Nigeria in December 15th 2008 (with Babatunde Ṣosan on piano), the final performance at the Liverpool Everyman Theatre on June 24th 2011 before its demolition for redevelopment, its Caribbean premiere at the Edna Manley School of the Arts in Kingston, Jamaica on February 4th, 2012 (with Maceo Kemp on piano), and at Carnegie Hall, New York on February 12th, 2012, the occasion of Tayọ Aluko's fiftieth birthday, again with Michael Conliffe on piano.

Credits for original performances:

Call Mr. Robeson. A life, with songs

Written and performed by	Tayọ Aluko.
Director & Dramaturg	Oluṣọla Oyelẹyẹ
Designer	Phil Newman
Sound Designers	David Darlington and Liam McDermott
Sound Engineering	Derek Murray
Lighting Design	Gareth Starkey
Recorded Percussion	Oludele Ọlaṣẹinde

Paul Robeson's words culled and adapted from various sources, including:

Here I Stand, by Paul Robeson (Beacon Press, 1998)
Paul Robeson Speaks: Writings, Speeches, Interviews, 1918 - 1974. Ed: Philip S. Foner (Citadel Press, 1978)
Paul Robeson, by Martin Bauml Duberman (New Press, 1995)
Othello by William Shakespeare
Paul Robeson: Tribute to An Artist (Documentary)
Narr:Sidney Poitier, Dir: St. Claire Bourne
Paul Robeson: Speak of Me As I Am (Documentary) dir: Rachel Hermans

Music (incidental and sung) includes:

Nobody Knows de Trouble Ah Seen (Trad)
Steal Away (Trad) Arr. H Burleigh
Ballad for Americans (Robinson)
Song of the Volga Boatmen (Trad)
We'll Keep a Welcome (Jones)
The Old Folks at Home (Foster)
Joshua Fit de Battle Ob Jericho (Trad) Arr. L Brown
Iwe Kiko (Trad)
Swing Low, Sweet Chariot (Trad)
An Eriskay Love Lilt (Trad)
Ol' Man River (Kern, Hammerstein)
Joe Hill (Robinson)
Didn't My Lord Deliver Daniel (Trad) Arr L Brown
Git on Board, Little Children (Trad)

Deep River (Trad)
Oh, Freedom (Trad)
We Shall Overcome (Trad)
Just A Wearyin' For You (Jacobs-Bond, Fisher)
Goin' Home (Dvorak, Fisher). Arr. Fisher

Tayọ Aluko. Writer, Performer. Tayọ was born in Nigeria, and now lives in Liverpool. He worked previously as an architect and property developer, with a special but frustrated interest in eco-friendly construction. He has fronted orchestras as baritone soloist in British concert halls, and has also performed lead roles in such operas and musicals as *Nabucco, Kiss Me Kate* and *Anything Goes. Call Mr. Robeson* won three awards at the London Ontario Fringe in June 2012 and Best Solo Show at the Stratford UK Fringe in June 2013. He has performed the play around the UK, Canada, Nigeria, Jamaica and the USA (including New York's Carnegie Hall in February 2012). His other piece titled *From Black Africa to the White House* - a talk about Black Political Resistance, illustrated with Spirituals, has also been performed on three continents. He researched, wrote and narrated to camera a piece on West African History before the Trans-Atlantic Slave Trade, which forms part of the permanent exhibit at Liverpool's International Slavery Museum. His 15-minute play, *Half Moon*, which also deals with ancient Africa, has been performed by young people several times in the UK. Tayọ initiated *The Paul Robeson Art Is A Weapon Festival* which was first staged at the Tristan Bates Theatre in London's Covent Garden in October 2013.

Olusọla Oyelẹyẹ, Director and Dramaturg. Olusọla is an award winning writer, director and producer working in opera, music theatre, visual arts and dance. Theatre includes: *A Wing, A Prey, A Song* (Guest Project Africa), *Moon Heaven* (Ariya UK tour), *Shanty Town* (Arvon

Foundation), Tin (The Lowry), *Ti-Jean and his Brothers* (Collective Artistes, National Theatre, Cottesloe), Resident Director on Trevor Nunn's West End production of *Porgy and Bess* (Savoy Theatre), Staff Producer at English National Opera, *Spirit of Okin* and *Sankofa* (Adzido Pan African Dance Ensemble, National & International tours), *Coming Up For Air* (The Drum & UK tour), *The Resurrection of Roscoe Powell* (Soho Theatre), The Shelter (RSC Barbican Theatre), Medea (Ariya, Royal National Theatre Studio), *The Playground* (Polka Theatre, Time Out Critics' Choice Pick of the Year), *High Life*, (Hampstead Theatre), *Maybe Father*, (Talawa, Young Vic), *Twelfth Night* (British Council Tour, Zimbabwe), *Ella*, a monodrama about Ella Fitzgerald (Rich Mix), *The Security Guard* (Tristan Bates). Opera includes: Akin Euba's *Orunmila's Voices: Songs from the Beginning of Time* (Jefferson Arts Centre, New Orleans), *Chaka: An Opera in Two Chants* with the St. Louis African Chorus, *Dido and Aeneas* (Ariya/Tricycle/BAC), *God's Trombones* (Fairfield Halls) and the second cast revival of Jonathan Miller's production of *The Mikado* (English National Opera). Oluṣọla has also worked as a director and educator in Ghana, South Africa, Zimbabwe, Nigeria, Hungary and the Czech Republic. She has been a visiting lecturer and Artist at Universities in South Africa and London, and was Head of the Acting Studio at Morley College. Her poetry has been set to music by Akin Euba and performed at both Harvard and Cambridge Universities. She is a Fellow of the Royal Society for the Arts.

Phil Newman, Designer & Assistant Director. Phil's Set & Costume Designs have featured in productions by companies as diverse as Ladder to the Moon, Trestle, Ariya, Full House Theatre, London Shakespeare Workout, Rouge28 Theatre and Impetuous Kinship. Recent credits include: UK & UAE tour of Shakespeare 4 Kidz' *The Tempest, Peter Pan* (Tickled Pink), *Dance or Die* (contemporary dance performance choreographed by Avant Garde's Tony Adigun), *Cinderella* (Library Theatre, Luton), *Voices in the Alleyway* and *Yes, I Still Exist* for Spread Expression Dance, Faith Drama's *The Fiddler* (Unicorn Theatre) & *Next Door* (Cockpit Theatre), *The Famous Five* (Tabard Theatre), Chalkfoot's acclaimed *The Riddle of the Sands* and *Laurel & Hardy* (Jermyn St Theatre, London & UK tours) as well as tours of *Queen Elizabeth's Elephant* and *The Ragged Trousered Philanthropists, Hansel & Gretel* (UK tour incl. Greenwich Theatre), *Stockholm* (BAC), and open-air tours of *The Merchant of Venice* and *The Railway Children* (Heartbreak Productions). Phil also designed the award-winning UK & international touring production of John Retallack's *Hannah & Hanna* (Time Out Critics' Choice). Other productions in collaboration with Oluṣọla Oyeleye include *The Security Guard, Ella* (RichMix), *High Life* (Hampstead Theatre), *Coming Up For Air* (UK tour), *Ma Joyce's Tales from the Parlour* (Oval House Theatre) and *The Playground* (Time Out Critics' Choice, London). He has just designed the Set for Theatre Giant's UK tour of *Houdini*.

Michael Conliffe, Piano & original/improvised Incidental Music Michael was born in Oldham, Greater Manchester and now lives in Leeds, West Yorkshire. He is a self-employed piano teacher to students of all ages, and jazz piano player performing in duos and bands. His introduction to music performance was playing in church, with strong roots in Gospel. He went on to study the art of Jazz Piano at Leeds College of Music and Liverpool Community College. He has played in various Jazz Festivals around the UK and considers performing in *Call Mr Robeson* at New York's Carnegie Hall to be his defining moment. Michael has also performed in other theatrical shows including *God Bless the Child: An Evening with Billie Holiday*.

Thanks to the following for their generous support towards the production of this script, and the inaugural Paul Robeson Art Is A Weapon Festival at the Tristan Bates Theatre at the Actors Centre, Covent Garden, London, at which Call Mr. Robeson was performed between September 30th and October 26th 2013.

Elite Donors:
Yẹle and Shirley Aluko
Ann and Tony Brooks
Muhammed Sanusi Daggash
Virginia and Ed Daniel
Chris and Glynn Hargreaves
Jack Heyman and Carol Canter
Ian McCartney
Yasmin Mohammed
Toyin Ọlawoye
Anonymous Donor
Dorothy Taylor

Premium Donors:
Bọsẹde Afọlabi
Caroline Baker
Ibrahim Chindo
Biọdun Eke-Aluko
Ralph Gibson, in memory of his father John
Amaju Ikomi
Patricia Kipping
Sandra Obiago
Ladipọ Onipẹde Jnr
Jane Weeks

Thanks also go to the following:
Aman Chara, John Dickens, Susan Fogarty, David Jones, Colin
Kenny, Stephen Ormond, Cathy Pound and Ben Wallis, Marika
Sherwood, Seattle Labor Chorus, Victoria (Canada) Friends of
Cuba

camp leaders

SUMMER CAMP JOBS IN THE USA

RETURN FLIGHTS TO THE USA ★ LIVE THE ★ **AMERICAN** ★ DREAM ★ NINE WEEK **SUMMER CAMP JOB** *Explore America* **GET PAID!**

MAKE THIS SUMMER COUNT

CAMPLEADERS.COM

FOLLOW ON FACEBOOK, TWITTER & INSTAGRAM   ONE OF MANY GREAT PROGRAMS BY smaller earth

Author's note

Thank you for picking up this publication.

Since Paul Robeson first introduced himself to me in Liverpool early one morning in June 1995, I have been on quite an incredible journey – one that I could not have imagined before then – taking me to many places I had never dreamed of going, or even heard of.

At each performance of the play, I try to do a welcome paragraph in the day or week's programme that relates Paul Robeson to what is happening in the world and/or locality at that time. That is always an interesting, and sometimes difficult challenge, and people have suggested on occasion that I might want to publish them . They are actually all online at callmrrobeson.com, and their publication on paper may or may not happen sometime in the future. For the purposes of this first edition of the script however, I have picked out three: one from Nigeria, one from New York and one from the West Coast of Canada. They not only demonstrate how far I have been privileged to take Mr. Robeson's story geographically, but also how constantly relevant his thoughts, ideas and life remain to us today, regardless of how much he has been sidelined by more famous figures.

The first was written a few days after I had introduced young Nigerian boys at my old school in Lagos to Robeson, the second was for the performance at that modest little venue known as Carnegie Hall in New York, where I performed on the occasion of my fiftieth birthday, and the last of the three was written barely a week before this script was submitted for publication. I think it perfectly sums up all that Robeson means – to me, and to the world.

Agip Hall, MUSON Centre, Lagos, Nigeria, Thursday September 28th, 2009

Greetings, and welcome. A few days ago, I had the wonderful experience of going back to my old school, King's College, to share the story of Paul Robeson with the current generation of "future leaders." Being on stage there some 32 years after leaving, and experiencing a standing ovation from a hall full of young men who naturally had not heard of Paul Robeson but now seemed genuinely moved and inspired by his story was particularly gratifying and poignant. Even though I and many who went before and since were once future leaders of our country, too many of whom have perhaps failed to carry out in full those words in our school song, urging us to pay "service to the living, honour to our dead," I can only hope that some of those young men, in learning about Paul Robeson, might be inspired to play their part in making a future Nigeria a better place than it is today. As for those of you here today, I hope that you will enjoy the performance, and yourselves be re-energised in whatever way you can, to "do the state some service."

Carnegie Hall, New York, February 12th, 2012

Greetings and Welcome. I had a dream (actually, it seemed more of a nightmare at the time) about eighteen or nineteen years ago. I was in a café opposite New York's Carnegie Hall, where I was scheduled to give a concert the following day. The people started to arrive by the hundreds, for my concert. But, they were a whole day early! I ran out of the café, waving my hands frantically, shouting, "Not today, not today! Come back tomorrow!" .... Then I woke up, sweating, heart pounding. Why I, then a lowly employed architect who happened to love singing, should picture myself centre- stage at Carnegie Hall is beyond me, but here I am, and I am happy to say that I got the right date!

Another story is worth retelling. The day was June 23 1995, the time approximately 6.30am. This architect was actually up and about, and believe it or not, singing in public. The Friends of Sefton Park Palm House in Liverpool were raising funds for the refurbishment of the famous landmark, which had lain derelict for decades. They had chosen to use the occasion of the Summer Solstice to hold an event called the Dawn Chorus, and I had been asked to sing. I chose what I thought to be an appropriate song: "My Lord, What a Morning". This lady came up to me afterwards and said, "You remind me of Paul Robeson. Do you sing many of his songs?" I think that may have been the first time I had heard his name, and I certainly didn't know his music. By chance (is that what it was?) I stumbled upon his biography two months later, read it, was amazed not just by his incredible story, but by the fact that it seemed to have been almost completely buried. I decided to do what I could to correct that, and here I am.

Robeson's story has been incredibly inspiring to me and to practically all that have heard it through me. Since 2007, I have performed it a few hundred times on four continents - to people from as young as seven to as old as one hundred and five! Everybody of course takes something different from it. For me it was two things. First was a pride in Africa. Thanks to his father, the Reverend William Drew Robeson, Paul and his siblings — even as far back as the turn of the last century, when racism in America was much greater than it is now — learnt about the real history of Africa, and found a pride in that history: a pride that is often hard for children of Africa to find and hold on to today.

The other thing was a belief in the power that lies within us as human beings – as individuals able to find strength in difficult times, or when people gather in large numbers to work for the common good, and achieve the seemingly unachievable. The American Civil Rights Movement that owes so much to people like Robeson, that gave a America its first Black President and allows us all to sit as equals in a place like Carnegie Hall without a second thought, is one example. Another is the South African Liberation Struggle – again, one that Robeson was a part of, even as far back as the 1930s. Such movements are almost as old as mankind. After a lull of a few decades, we are seeing people waking up in all corners of the earth, rising up and demanding change. Robeson would, I am sure, be with those who are rediscovering this strength in mass action – from the streets of the Middle East to the squares in the many cities and towns around America and elsewhere around the world, the people having decided that things just cannot be allowed to continue the way they have for so long. And even when governments and politicians unleash the might of their armed forces on these people whose only crime is to dream of peace, justice and equality (the powers-that-be in American cities appear no less guilty than the tyrants elsewhere) the bravery of the people remains incredible and awe-inspiring.

Paul Robeson's talent, achievements and example are similarly awe-inspiring, and I am grateful that he chose to reveal his story to me, and inspired me to share that story around the world. I am always gratified by the reactions to that story, and hope that it continues to inspire people to join the fight for freedom, peace and justice worldwide, and most importantly, to keep dreaming.

Greetings and Welcome. It is said that had Mahalia Jackson, who had earlier sung "I been 'buked, an' I been scorned" not called out, "Tell 'em about the dream, Martin!" we might not have been commemorating the August 1963 March on Washington in the last few weeks. She is not the only one to thank for transforming a remarkable event into a historic one - there were hundreds who had organised the event behind the scenes, and there were the thousands who had made long journeys across the land to create and inspire that great moment. There were also the many who had gone before, including hundreds of thousands who had made the even longer, more dangerous and arduous journeys north to places like Halifax in the days of slavery, as well as the many often nameless ones who either sheltered them or guided them along the way. Many continue to exhibit such bravery around the world today, even in Dr. King's country, such as those who are prepared to sacrifice their liberty by exposing truths that their government would prefer to keep hidden from the people. These people join a long line of political prisoners (which includes many forgotten, ageing - and sometimes dying - Black Panthers and other freedom fighters) who are prepared to pay a high price for standing up and shouting out against injustices and abuses of power. In his time, Paul Robeson did just that, and if ever there was someone who was "'buked and scorned," it was he. It is surely beholden upon the rest of us to continue the work of these great, brave people, for we know that even though we have climbed a few rungs up that metaphorical ladder to the promised land that King and his ancestors and forerunners had dreamed of, we seem to be constantly climbing a few rungs back down into the abyss of inhumanity, and if we don't keep pushing together from behind, we do a disservice to those who paved the way for us to have the freedoms and privileges we enjoy today.

Thanks.

Paul Robeson's name has opened so many doors for me around the world, and there are far too many people to thank for their help in taking the story to so many places, and reaching so many people. You all know who you are, and I thank you. Closest of all to the project were the creative team comprising Oluṣọla Oyelẹyẹ (who saw the potential in the first – now quite embarrassing – draft I sent to her), and dramaturged, guided and directed me through the creative process, Phil Newman whose design ideas helped shape the play, and Michael Conliffe, whose instinctive musicianship, quiet understanding, patience and companionship as we toured to the remotest parts of the British Isles and beyond were a rock for me. I would also like to single out Bonnie Weiss of Emeryville, California - the researcher and archivist for the Bay Area Paul Robeson Centennial Committee for all her help – from proof-reading my newsletters and programme notes to chauffeuring me around the Bay Area, opening doors for me, and for doing more than just about anybody else I can think of to keep Robeson's name alive.

Tayọ Aluko

Team at Carnegie Hall, February 2013.
L - R: Michael Conliffe, Olusola Oyeleye, Tayo Aluko, Phil Newman

Don't need to be there @ Carnegie Hall
by Carol Rosegg

The un-Americans by Sarah Franklin

In the Mid-1940s by Tom Hart

Director's Note

Now faith is the assurance of things hoped for, the conviction of things not seen.

Hebrews 11:1

The play that Tayọ Aluko gave me to read was not the powerful monodrama that we eventually shaped together. That first version of the script was a theatrical opus worthy, in scenes, of a National Theatre production. It was a costume drama exploring the life of Paul Robeson, his connection with Liverpool, an African Spirit Mother and Liverpool's participation in the Atlantic Slave Trade. A play with music, it had a large cast of fifteen or so characters and, it was political with a capital 'P': a great effort for a first play. Wearing my dramaturge's hat, I could see the potential for a powerful one man play with music, exploring and honouring a period in the rich life of Paul Robeson. The journey from page to stage has been a long one requiring resilience, patience and faith. The saying that behind every successful man is a very strong woman, is definitely pertinent in this creative setting: since guiding a first-time writer towards creating a structure that tells a complex, but finely tuned story, and as the director, showcasing the performance skills of the singer/actor, particularly when the writer is the performer, is a creative challenge. It took some persuading.

This is a role for a skilled singer. It requires stamina and performance dexterity to shift between the bass-baritone singing voice, the oratory voice of the public speeches and the intimate storytelling of the private domain. Call Mr Robeson explores the public and private worlds of Paul Robeson, husband, father, part-time lawyer, world renowned entertainer and political activist, whose fight for political and social justice for all disenfranchised peoples lead to US government surveillance. He was called before the House Committee on Un-American Activities (HUAC), and although his fight for civil rights predates and overlaps the activism Malcolm X, Dr Martin Luther King Jr and others: he is largely ignored or forgotten. This and other factors eventually impacted on his health.

In the first and last scenes we see Paul Robeson enter carrying the 'heavy load'. I drew on the themes of isolation, misrepresentation and burdens - the dissonance between the private and public worlds, the fact that different organisations hold intimate details about each of us, and the notion of how mental distress can impact perception, - in discussions with the designer Phil Newman, initially to create a room full of box files that held Paul Robeson's 'life'. Phil's almost forensic passion for being 'in the period', lead to a design that allows the audience to discover Paul Robeson as if stumbling into a room strewn with box files, on top of a broken record, sharing fragments of his life, his work, his spirituality.

Developing the script for Call Mr Robeson and directing the play has been an enjoyable creative journey, underscored by a strong unwavering belief that the monodrama was the appropriate structure to tell this story. As creative people, we should always draw from the

Source and be steadfast in our convictions to tell our stories by every means possible.

Finally I need to acknowledge the following people: Tayọ Aluko for his courage and determination; Paul Robeson Jr and his wife Marilyn for their graciousness, for taking the time to speak with me in Liverpool and New York. Getting by with a little help from your friends and family is a true dictum: so thank you Garry A Morris for offering your house in Birmingham as a space to work at a crucial time in the creative process. I also thank my mother, Mrs W O Oyelẹyẹ with all my heart, for reminding me often that: when God says yes, no one can say no. It has been a powerful mantra on this journey.

Oluṣọla Oyelẹyẹ

August 2013

Dedicated to the memory of:

My late Brother
Bankọle Olumide Aluko (Senior Advocate of Nigeria)
Who, when he played King Lear at King's College Lagos in
1974 had me play his daughter, Goneril.
I confirm that that was the last time I ever wore a dress...
In public... or private!

My late Mother
Janet Adebisi Aluko (nee Fajẹmisin)
Who made me enter the Unilag Staff School Choir (no ifs,
no buts) at the age of seven.
Thank you for setting me on the road.

My late Father
Dr. Timothy Mofọlọrunṣọ Aluko
Who, after seeing Call Mr. Robeson in Lagos in October
2008, dropped his reservations and said to me, "If you
want to do this full time, you have my blessing."

And
My late business partner
Andrew David Brooks
Whose exit from this earth opened, by a few more degrees,
the door that would see me enter my own new world.

CHARACTERS

PAUL ROBESON

Black man. Large of stature. Singer with an excellent bass or baritone voice. Playing age, 30s to 70s.

LAWRENCE (LARRY) BROWN

Robeson's longest serving pianist and arranger. Also a black man. (Note: this part is non-speaking and the race and sex of the pianist are therefore not fixed.) An ability to improvise in the black gospel style would be an advantage.

Preset: LARRY BROWN at piano, USR, playing a medley of spirituals and other Robeson songs, as audience files in. The set consists of file cases littered around the stage, amid paraphernalia relating to Robeson's life: photographs, papers, film, play and concert tour posters etc (Note: where appropriate, permission to be obtained for what is displayed on stage) and lots of books. Lights fade to black, and piano stops. The sound of an old fashioned needle hitting a record is heard. PAUL starts to sing off stage, a cappella.

Nobody knows de trouble I seen
(Enters USL carrying a chair)
Nobody knows my sorrow
Nobody knows de trouble I seen
Glory Hallelujah

He places the chair SC as he finishes, puts reading glasses on. Sound of vinyl record stops. LARRY starts to play the introduction to OL' MAN RIVER. PAUL begins to sing, in rehearsal.

(Sings) Niggers all work on de Mississippi
Niggers all work while de white folk play
Pulling dem boats from de dawn till sunset
Gettin' no rest till...

(He starts to address the audience as LARRY stops.)

There I was, rehearsing with Larry, and my wife
Essie barges in, just like that, and asks me, 'Paul!

Paul, Paul Robeson, don't you think it's about time you stopped singing that darn song?' And I say, 'Darn? Dar- Essie, that song was written for me!' (To audience) You know, for the role of Joe in Showboat. And she says, 'Yes, by a white massa for his favourite nigger. Niggers this, Niggers that. How can you carry on singing those words and expect to be taken seriously?' Well, "my dearly beloved" had her faults, but a lack of expressive clarity wasn't one of them! And I say, 'Listen, Eslanda, "that darn song" is the reason I am famous today and why many white folks now show me – and therefore you – respect. Honey, don't you see that I can use music to show that we are equal to them?' Then she says quietly, 'Not by letting them carry on calling us niggers, you won't', and then she changes the subject, and starts to talk about arrangements and fees for my next concert. You see, she was my manager too, and a darn good one at that. Well, I refuse to stop singing "that darn song", but I do change the lyrics...

(*Sings*)
"Coloured folks work on de Mississippi, Coloured folks work while de white folks play..."

She's still not that happy about it, and I decide I'll probably stop singing it after a few years. But then, about a year or so after that, Essie announces out of the blue, that she has agreed a fee of forty thousand dollars for me to play the role in the movie. In Hollywood! Forty Thousand dollars! Just for a few scenes, and that's in 1935! The rest, as they say, is history. (*Beat. Chuckles*) To think that I was ready to stop singing "that darn song".

There had been somebody else before I met Essie. Gerry Neale, her name was. My first true love. (*Finds photo USR and walks DSR with it*) We met while I was at Rutgers College in New Jersey, and she was in teacher training at Trenton... I asked her to marry me several times. She thought about it for a long time, but eventually she said, 'Look, I ain't strong enough to marry you, Paul Robeson. Something about you tells me that I'd be marrying nothing but trouble.' (*Chuckles. Beat*) I guess she was right. (*Beat. Returns photo USR and moves DSC*)

Anyway, when I went to Columbia University to study law, I carried on with my football. As a matter of fact, I had been in the All-American team in 1917 and 1918. Even as a teenager, I was already famous! All over the country, people knew me as "Robey of Rutgers." One reporter even described me as "Six foot four and two hundred graceful pounds of dark devastation." Well, at Columbia, I got this serious injury on my thigh, and needed to spend some weeks at the New York

Presbyterian Hospital. That's where I met Eslanda Cardoso Goode. Essie. (*Picks up photo*) Fine, small woman. Spirited. Vivacious. And, the only coloured woman on the senior staff. Well, being so fair, she could often pass for white. By the time they found out, it was clearly too late!

When we decided to get married, we discovered that her family weren't best pleased. Turns out I was too... dark, see? My brother Ben wasn't so sure about her either. He thought her too ambitions, too abrasive. Still, we were in love, and that was that: we married anyway. (*Replaces photo*) I was 23, she was 26. August 1921. (*Sits. Beat*)

Six years later, we had a boy. Paul Jnr. Pauli. Great kid. Smart. I'm afraid I wasn't around much for him, especially when he was small. Always on the road, see? And even when I wasn't touring, well, truth is, Essie and I, we didn't always get along too well together, and I'd often pitch up in hotels, or with friends, and I felt comfortable doing that. With her, it was always - passports, concerts, "sing this, don't sing that. I've booked you on this, your fee is this, my cut is that. Read this script, but don't take that part." (*Beat*) Don't get me wrong: she was a lovely, beautiful, thoughtful woman - a great mother to Pauli. But you see, for me, home is where one goes to be at peace, where you can just... Be... Just think... Rest, you know?

Talk about – anything, or nothing. (*Beat*) Still, we did have lots of good times together. We'd walk in the garden, read, talk, go out to the theatre, I'd play football with Pauli. You know, family stuff. And Essie's mom – Ma Goode – she was around much of the time to help look after Pauli, because I wasn't there... Or was I not there because she was?

No, I admit I probably wasn't the best of fathers. Not like my Pop. The Reverend William Drew Robeson. Now, there was a man! (*Rises and goes searching for photo*) He raised all five of us almost single-handedly, after my... after my mother died... In a fire. I was... I was there – (*Beat*) I was... just six years old. (*Beat. Continues searching*) Pop was a preacher, with this big, booming voice. He always, always had this dignity about him that even white folks just had to admire and respect. (*Finds photo*) It was he who encouraged me to stay on in the Rutgers football team when I was ready to quit, because I was made to know I was not welcome. I'll never forget when I first showed up for the team trial. The very first scrimmage, both sides just went for me, because I was colored! Both sides! I got a sprained shoulder, cuts and bruises all over, a spike in my hand, my fingernails ripped off... Ten days I was laid up in bed after that, ten days! Of course, I wanted to quit. But Pop impressed on me that as the only coloured kid at Rutgers, I was the representative of a whole lot of Negro boys who wanted to go to college, who wanted to play football, and I had to show that I was ready to take whatever was handed out. And with his coaching, I became a Phi Beta Kappa scholar, and a prize-winning orator. (*Beat*)

Three days before my last oratorical contest... Pop died. (*Piano starts to play introduction to STEAL AWAY*) But I still entered it, and I won! He would have been so proud...

(*Sings*)

Steal away, steal away, steal away to Jesus
Steal away, steal away home
I ain't got long to stay here.

My Lord calls me, he calls me by the thunder
The trumpet sounds within a my soul
I ain't got long to stay here.

Steal away, steal away, steal away to Jesus
Steal away, steal away home
I ain't got long to stay here.

(*Piano continues to play to the end of this next section*)

What a beautiful, dignified song! (*Rises*) You know, it was originally sung as a secret code for slaves getting ready to escape, so for me it encapsulates Pop's life, because he was actually born in slavery in Martin County, North Carolina, but at the age of fifteen he escaped North, to a better place. (*Music out*) (*Beat*)

Many times, I also escaped to what I thought was a better place: Russia. (*Piano starts to play THE SONG OF THE VOLGA BOATMEN*) From the time I first visited there in 1934, I found that their folk songs bore a close relationship to those of the Negro people, and that a tremendous bond of sympathy and mutual understanding united us. In Russia, I was treated like a full human being for the first time in my life. There was no racial prejudice! So I – we – sent Pauli to school there, when he was nine. We felt it would be better for him to grow up in a non-racial, socialist country, rather than in America, where he would always be a second-class citizen. (*Piano out*)

Now, I first got interested in Socialism in Britain in the 1920s. One night, during the run of Showboat at the Theatre Royal, Drury Lane in London I was coming out of this exclusive restaurant, and was drawn by the sound of a group of men singing on the street. It turns out they were coal miners, from a place called, er, Wales. These

fellows had marched hundreds of miles to London
– in winter – to highlight their plight: they'd been
working in very dangerous, unhealthy conditions,
for immensely rich bosses, on wages that could
barely feed them, let alone their families. You
know, I actually bought them their first hot meal
in days! It actually shocked me to discover that in
a white country there could be such a wide divide
between the ruling elite and the working class.

I soon came to realise that the same capitalist
system that uprooted Africans from their home,
kept them at the bottom of the pile in America,
operated in Europe too! ... and that the fascists
would do anything in their power to crush any
resistance. Take Spain in the 1930s. I participated
in a concert in support of the Republican refugees
at the Royal Albert Hall, London, June 1937.

(*Steps on 'podium'*)

"I am deeply happy to be joining with you in this
appeal for the greatest cause which faces the world
today. Like every true artist, I have longed to see
my talent contributing in an unmistakably clear
manner to the cause of humanity. The challenge
must be taken up. Fascism is no respecter of
persons. It makes no distinction between
combatants and non-combatants. The blood-
soaked streets of Guernica are proof of that, as are

38

the concentration camps full of artists and scientists. The liberation of Spain from the oppression of fascist reactionaries is not a private matter of the Spaniards, but the common cause of all advanced and progressive humanity. The artist must take sides. He must elect to fight for freedom or slavery. I have made my choice. I had no alternative."

(*Steps down*)

Yes, I had choices to make, alright. You see, in London in 1929, I'd met this very beautiful woman. Yolande Jackson. She was white. From a wealthy, aristocratic family. We fell deeply, deeply in love, and decided to get married, even though I knew that if I divorced Essie for a white woman, folks back home would never forgive me. Not the Negroes, and definitely not the whites. But love is an irresistible force, and so I asked Essie to initiate divorce proceedings and name Yolande as correspondent. In the end however, Yolande's father absolutely forbade her from marrying a Negro, and she relented. I was devastated at first, but eventually I came to terms with it, and Essie and I resolved to stay together, which we did.

(*Sits*)

I had choices to make about my movie career too.

You see, in England, I could get to play starring roles in a way that was totally impossible for a Negro actor in America back then. But it came at a price, because after filming, and thus unbeknownst to me, many of the movies would be edited in a way that would make my character look like he was venerating the white man. Worst of all was Chief Bosambo in Sanders of the River. Ah ee yo ko! Ah ee yo ko! The least said about him, the better! On the other hand I did get to play some pretty good roles, like The Emperor Jones, and David Goliath, in The Proud Valley. That was filmed in Wales, with real Welsh miners. (*Sings*) Lord God of Abraham! And during filming I actually stayed in their homes, with their families. I'd never felt so happy, so comfortable. So – loved. Goliath was just a regular working class fellow, but a real hero. Yes – definitely my best movie, but waiting for roles like that to come along was like waiting for the freedom train itself.

And then I had to decide whether to continue supporting International Peace and Socialist causes, or just entertain. My London agent warned me that my political activities might adversely affect my career. And you know what? That year I polled first place – get that – first place – among BBC listeners, as "The most popular singer on radio." And I sold out the Royal Albert Hall and countless venues all around Britain too, so he was clearly plain wrong.

(*Rises*)

And then, back home in America a few years later, I recorded a very patriotic song called The Ballad for Americans, (*Piano starts to play THE BALLAD FOR AMERICANS*) and boy, did that make me big!

(Sings)

Ol' Abe Lincoln was thin and long
His heart was high and his faith was strong
But he hated oppression, he hated wrong
And he went down to his grave to free the slave...

(*Piano continues*)

It was played on every radio station the length and breadth of the country! I toured all over, singing it with orchestras and choirs. That was definitely the peak of my popularity, and of my career, commercially. (*Piano stops*) Everywhere I went, my concerts were packed. (*Piano starts playing introduction to THE OLD FOLKS AT HOME*) I remember singing one night in Kansas City sometime in 1942, the Municipal Auditorium:

(*Steps onto "stage" DSC*)

Way down upon de Swanee Ribber
Far, far away
Dere's where my heart is turning ever
Dat's where the old folks stay

(*He starts to peer into the audience as he continues*)

All around am sad an' dreary
Everywhere I roam

Oh, fellas, how my heart grows weary...

(*He stops singing, and piano stops soon after*)

Excuse me, ladies and gentlemen, but I – can I have the house lights on please? (*The sound of a restless audience is heard. He looks round the audience, and then up into where the circle would be. Sound fades as he starts to speak*)
I have been going round the country for several years now, and everywhere I've been, I have campaigned tirelessly for equal rights for my people, for our integration at all levels of society. I have also insisted that I will not sing to segregated audiences. I thought that that had been understood by the management of this auditorium when this concert was arranged, but I see that their pledge has not been honoured, because we have white people down here, and Negro people up there. For this reason, I'm afraid I have to say

that this concert is now over.

(*Walks purposefully USR. pauses, then turns to address audience*)

You see, only the previous week, I had sung The Ballad for Americans at the Hollywood Bowl, with the biggest damn orchestra and chorus you can imagine...

(*Sings*)

Man in white skin can never be free while his black brother is in slavery.

30,000 people cheering me to kingdom come. And you know what? That night at my hotel, they told me I could not eat in the restaurant, that the guests would not approve! I had to eat upstairs in my room with Freda – er, that's Freda Diamond - a, er, close friend. So when I encountered this segregated audience in Kansas City, I figured, enough's enough, and I walked right off that stage into the dressing room, and as far as I was concerned, that was that. Then the manager walks in, all arrogant, talking about suing me and all, and I told him I'd see him in court. I had to take a stand, see? He had the good sense to get the hell out of there. Then the compère comes in with these two other fellows, but he's begging me, explaining that the manager was new. He goes out on stage (I can hear him from the dressing room):

(*At CS, adopting the Compère's voice*)

"Excuse me, ladies and gentlemen – and this includes our – friends – upstairs. We apologise for this unfortunate misunderstanding.

The management is in talks with Mr Robeson right now, and we are hoping that he might be persuaded to rejoin us just as soon as possible."

Eventually, I calm down, and I decide to go back out there. But I lay it down straight.

(*Steps back up to stage, to the sound of the audience enthusiastically welcoming him back. He raises his hands to ask for silence, then speaks*)

I see that Jim Crow is alive and well in Kansas City tonight, and you know my views. However, I feel that my people upstairs, who have paid good hard-earned money to hear me sing tonight must not be disappointed, so I will continue with this concert, but for their sake only. Let there be no doubt that I am continuing only under protest. I will therefore sing, for my people upstairs, songs of our people's struggle, for we have resisted hundreds of years of slavery, but continue to fight

44

injustice, continue to have to battle to preserve our dignity. (*Beat. Points towards exit*) Yes, Sir, Madam, you may leave if you wish, and be sure to ask for a refund on your way out. Larry, Battle of Jericho, please.

(*LARRY plays, PAUL sings*)

> Joshua fit de battle ob Jericho,
> Jericho, Jericho
> Joshua fit de battle ob Jericho
> An' de walls come a tumbling down
>
> You may talk about your King ob Gideon
> You may talk about your man ob Saul
> Dere's none like Good ol' Joshua
> At de battle ob Jericho
>
> Up to de walls ob Jericho
> He marched wid sword in han'
> Go blow dem ram horns Joshua cried
> Cause de battle am in my hand
>
> Den de lam' ram sheep horns begin to blow
> An de trumpets begin to soun'
> Joshua commanded de chillun to shout
> An de walls come a tumbling down
> Dat mornin'

Joshua fit de battle ob Jericho
Jericho, Jericho
Joshua fit de battle ob Jericho
An' de walls come a tumbling down

(*Leaves "stage"*)

Always makes me think of Frederick Douglass,
that song. A great leader in the freedom struggles
of my people. A nineteenth century Joshua. Like
Pop, he also escaped slavery by the Underground
Railroad. He visited Europe in 1849, and in a
farewell speech to the British people, he said this:

"I go back to the United States not as I landed
here – I came a slave – and I go back a free man. I
came here maligned, I go back with reputation and
celebrity. Still, I go back to toil. I do not go back
to America to sit still, remain quiet and enjoy ease
and comfort. I prefer living a life of activity in the
service of my brethren."

Amen to that! (*Beat*) He wrote a wonderful
autobiography, you know: "The Narrative of the
Life of Frederick Douglass, an American Slave,"
and I own a copy autographed by him almost a
century and a half ago! That's one of the prize
items in my book collection. Oh, I love books, I
love reading. That's why travelling so much has
never been a problem for me. You see, I say:

"thousands of miles only means dozens of books." I've got hundreds, on all sorts of subjects, from African History to world religions; music and musicology to linguistics and languages. You know, I can now converse quite fluently in maybe, twenty-five languages: including Russian, Yiddish, Mandarin Chinese, and some African ones, like Efik and Swahili. I've just got this hunger, this thirst, a yearning for learning, for knowledge, see?

(He discovers a newspaper cutting in the book he's holding. He picks it up, remembers it)

Listen to this: "Paul Robeson says..." No. Wait a minute. *(Puts book and clipping down)* I'll let you hear what I actually said, and then I'll read the clipping to you. I'm in Europe in 1949, and like Frederick Douglass, I speak out on behalf of my people. And I always like to say things that relate American Negroes to Europeans, like in Liverpool, I said to a small gathering there once:

I need to draw attention of people here in Europe to what's happening in my country. I stand here ashamed to be an American. Ashamed that 87 full years after Abraham Lincoln signed the Emancipation Proclamation, it is still necessary to speak of the wave of lynch terror and mob assault against Negro Americans. Lynching is not the special or exclusive concern of Negro Americans.

The good Aryan who stood idly by while the German Jew was being persecuted lived to learn that that was the beginning of the end of his own freedom. Let us not some day live to learn that the persecution of the Negro was the beginning of the end of all American freedom.

(*To audience*)

And then at the World Peace Congress in Paris, France that April, I made the speech that changed everything.

(*Steps back onto podium*)

"The wealth of America was built on the backs of white workers from Europe and on the backs of millions of blacks, and we are resolved to share it equally among our children. And we shall not put up with any hysterical raving that urges us to make war on anyone. We shall not make war on the Soviet Union. It is unthinkable that American Negroes would go to war on behalf of those who have oppressed us for generations against a country which in one generation has raised our people to the full dignity of mankind."

(*Pause. Steps off podium*)

You know how they reported that speech back in

the United States? (*Reads the clipping*) "Paul Robeson says that no intelligent Negro would fight for the United States as it presently exists"... "He describes the policies of the United States government as being no different to those of Hitler and Goebbels."

Well! That was the beginning of the end of my own freedom. I get back to America and all hell breaks loose. Right from the time I get off the plane, the press is there waiting for me. (*The sound of a melée of reporters and flashing cameras is heard, followed by questions addressed to PAUL*)

REPORTER: Mr Robeson, you are reported as denouncing your government in Paris. What do you have to say for yourself?

PAUL: I prefer to give what I have to say to papers like The Daily Worker.

REPORTER: Did you not say that you loved Russia more than any other country?

PAUL: I said that I love the America of the working class. And I love the working class of England and France and many other countries. And I very deeply love the people's republics in Eastern Europe and the Soviet Union, for their fight for freedom for my people and for the white working people of the world."

REPORTER: What do you think of President Truman's fight for civil rights?

PAUL: President Truman is merely promising, but not giving, the Negro people privileges, not rights. The privilege of not being lynched."

REPORTER: Mr Walter White of the NAACP denounced your Paris speech as unpatriotic. What do you say to that, Mr Robeson?

(*Beat. To audience*)

> Now, I wasn't expecting that one and I really have to think quick. It's like I'm back on the football field. You see, despite my size, I was very quick, and I could do these amazing sidesteps. Some fellows would be coming for me, and next moment (*Does a sidestep*), I'd be someplace else. So I say, 'If Mr White had read the truth about what I actually said in Paris, and not the distorted lies you printed, he would have understood that I am as patriotic as he or any other American, Negro or white. Now if you will excuse me I would like to get back home to my people in Harlem.'

(*To audience*)

> I thought I handled that quite well, but I was worried. You see, it's one thing to take abuse from

50

the white press or from whites in general, but the National Association for the Advancement of Coloured People? I'd been a supporter all my life! And then I find out that they'd been saying even worse things about me, which made me mad. Real mad! So I say to their committee, "How dare you, you errand boys, you Uncle Toms, challenge my Americanism? Most black Americans are not afraid of their radicals who point out the awful, indefensible truth of our degradation and exploitation, unlike you - you craven, fawning, despicable so called leadership!" (*Beat. To audience*) I don't think they liked that very much.

I speak here, there and everywhere: I'm really worried for my country, see? My people are still getting lynched, the workers exploited, trade unionists persecuted, the war mongers are spreading fear all over the place while they're quietly and secretly raping my brothers and sisters in Africa, Latin America and the Caribbean. Meanwhile the House Un-American Activities Committee is looking for "reds" under every bed: putting people on trial and in jail. Making them name names: real communists, people they think may be communists — mostly just regular honest liberals, progressives. (*Looks behind him as though hearing a voice*) What? (*Continues*) So I have to keep going, keep fighting for the working people. Keep battling, but there's so much happening:

51

Pauli's getting married, people are holding welcome rallies for me, some say I should run for Vice President, and Essie and Pauli, and – (*Looks round again, disconcerted*) and everybody's really worried about me, but I just have to keep going.

(*Beat*)

And then I've got this outdoor concert to do in a park in Peekskill, upstate New York. It's in aid of the Harlem Chapter of the Civil Rights Congress. I arrive there by train, and Helen is there to – er, that's er, Helen Rosen – another er, close friend – she's there to meet me, with her husband Sam, and we travel in their car. We get near the park, and there's trouble. (*The sound of a rioting mob is heard*) Seems some marauding white youths have blocked the road, are shouting at people and threatening them. Some are throwing rocks and stones at people's cars! The police are just standing there, watching, doing nothing! I'm so angry, I want to get out of the car and show them hell. But then Helen spots an effigy of me hanging from a tree, and yells – 'Paul! Stay in the car! Sam let's go! Let's get the hell out of here!' So Sam reverses the car all the way down the line, (*Moves SR*) we drive away, and the concert doesn't happen. (*Sound fades. Beat*)
Well, we decide to reschedule it for the following week. September 4. This time, the trade unions

send men to guard me and the concert goers. I travel laid down on the floor of a car, in a convoy, all of them with blackened windows. I was told it was necessary. I get out, and these big – well, big – trade unionists escort my accompanist, Larry Brown, and me up on stage, and form a circle around us (*Steps onto podium amid the sound of a cheering crowd*) There must be twenty thousand people out there. I see a ring surrounding the crowd. I stare, and then I realise what it is I'm seeing! A human chain of trade unionists: black men, white men, Asians, Latinos, all standing together, to protect us from the rioters out there. It's so moving! The crowd are all up on their feet. They're cheering so loud that Larry and I have to wait. Eventually we start, and we do a few songs. (*LARRY plays a bit of DEEP RIVER tentatively*) I can tell that poor Larry is terrified, from the way he's playing. Well, there had been talk of snipers out there in the hills somewhere. And there's a helicopter – a police helicopter – hovering in the distance, and I wonder if that's where the sniper might be? (*DEEP RIVER stops*) And as Larry starts to play the opening notes to our final number, (*Piano plays introduction to OL' MAN RIVER*) the helicopter starts coming towards us.

(*Sound of helicopter approaching, then circling during the song*)

Dere's an ol' man called de Mississippi
Dat's de ol' man I don't like to be
What does he care if de world's got troubles
What does he care if de land ain't free?

Ol' man river, dat ol' man river
He must know somethin' but don't say nothing
He just keeps rollin' he keeps on rollin' along.

He don't plant taters, he don't plant cotton
An' dem that plants 'em is soon forgotten
But ol' man river, he just keeps rollin' along.

You an' me, we sweat an' strain
Body all achin' and racked wid pain.
'Tote dat barge! Lift dat bale!'
You show a little grit an' you lands in jail

Ah keeps laughin' instead of cryin'
Ah must keep fightin' until I'm dyin'
But ol' man river, he just keeps rollin, along!

(*The helicopter sound fades out. Beat. PAUL steps down*)

There were worse riots after the concert. Again, the
police did nothing. Dozens of cars were damaged,
one hundred forty-five people got injured,
including one coloured man who lost an eye. All
because of me.

(Sits SL)

Then the papers say things like "ROBESON: THE EPITOMY OF THE COMMUNIST THREAT;" "CRAZY COMMIE CROWD WRECK PEACEFUL PEAKSKILL."

Things get even worse. Stores stop selling my records. The studios cancel my contracts. More and more people from all sides want less and less to do with me, and I start losing bookings and venues. Only a few churches – black churches – host my concerts, but soon, many of them start closing their doors on me too, afraid they'd lose their mortgages, or even get burned down. In the mid 1940s I could earn one hundred thousand dollars a year, easy. In 1955, I earned six thousand dollars. Six thousand! I'd do better abroad - in Europe. But then what does my government do? They place travel restrictions on me, and eventually in 1950, they cancel my passport altogether! They won't even let me go into Canada! Imagine! But then, the trade unions hit on a great idea. (*Stands. Moves to CS*) We held a concert at the border, under the Peace Arch. (*The sound of a large, cheering crow is heard*) Twenty-five to thirty thousand people show up – I'm on this side of the border in America, they on the other, starting just about where you are right now

55

(Pointing to front row. Steps up to address crowd. They quieten as he starts to speak)

Comrades. I can't act or sing in any sort of decent place in my own country. And yet, the British actors have sent a request saying that they would welcome me in England to play Othello. And at the same time, I have received an invitation *(Piano starts to play WE'LL KEEP A WELCOME IN THE HILLSIDES)* and no invitation could mean more - from the workers, the miners in Wales, where I first understood the struggle of Negro and White together - to appear at a festival over there in October, and I very much hope to be able to get there to do that. *(Piano stops)* But our government is preventing artists, and scientists, like Dr Du Bois, proudly a son of the Negro people, who has contributed to the advancement of all mankind, they are preventing him from leaving this country to attend peace meetings or scientific gatherings – anywhere on earth. And the same goes for countless outstanding American scientists, intellectuals, workers and trade union leaders too.

And as for me – why do they take my passport away? They said that I have been struggling for the independence of the colonial peoples of Africa, and that that is meddling in the foreign affairs of the United States government. Now that's just too bad, 'cause I'm going to have to continue to meddle! And I want everybody in the range of my voice to hear – official or otherwise – that there is no force on earth that will make me go backward one-thousandth part of one little inch!

(*Crowd cheers. Exhaustion descends on him heavily, briefly, but he perks up again. Appeals for quiet*)

And now, comrades, brothers and sisters, Joe Hill.

(*LARRY gives opening note to JOE HILL*)

(Sings)

> I dreamed I saw Joe Hill last night
> Alive as you and me.
> Says I, but Joe, you're ten years dead,
> I never died, says he,
> I never died, says he.
>
> The copper bosses killed you Joe,
> They shot you Joe, says I.
> Takes more than guns to kill a man.
> Says Joe, I didn't die.
> Says Joe, I didn't die.

Joe Hill ain't dead, he says to me,
Joe Hill ain't never died.
Where workers strike and organise,
Joe Hill is at their side,
I never died says he
I never died says he

(*Steps down*)

Nine years, that went on. Nine years under house arrest, unable to sing, act or travel, but I couldn't stop fighting. (*Sits in chair, CS*) I went to court several times, to protest the cancellation of my passport. Got nowhere. Oh, I knew that all they wanted was for me to say that I was a communist, and to give them some names. They would have thrown them in jail, and I would have been able to carry on singing, start earning again. But I couldn't do that. (*The sound of a scratching record is heard. He looks round*) What? (*Beat. To audience, whispering*) Oh, I forgot to warn you. They follow me around, you know – the FBI. Read my mail, keep files on me, they bug me – oh yes – they've probably been listening to this all night, but don't you worry, just don't say a word, but be careful who's sitting behind you. (*Behind*) What??

They visit me, tell me they've got tapes: Tapes of me in bed – with Helen, Freda, Clara, Uta, Peggy, whoever, but I keep going, because too many people are giving in, see? But Lord knows, I'm getting tired. Tired of fighting. Tired of swimming against the tide. Of climbing up a mountain and rocks keep falling on me. Tired of shouting into the wilderness and nobody's hearing, or even listening, but I keep going! (*Another scratching record is heard. Beat*) Did I ever tell you about the pentatonic scale? I've been studying the subject for a while now. It's fascinating. Basically, people's music - folk music - from any part of the world is instinctively based on just five notes, and they just happen to be the five black keys of the piano. Listen to this.

(*He goes over to the piano. LARRY freezes as PAUL stands next to him, plays the pentatonic scale*)

The five black keys of the piano. The pentatonic scale.

(*Sings and plays few bars of Iwe Kiko*)

Iwe kiko
lai si oko
Ati ada
Ko I pe o
Ko I pe o

That's Iwe Kiko, a Yoruba folk song taught to me by a Nigerian fellow student while we were studying in at London University in the 1930s. Every one of those notes you just heard is one of the five black keys of the piano. The pentatonic scale! Listen to this one:

(*Sings and plays*)

Swing low, sweet chariot
(*LARRY takes up the accompaniment*)
Coming for to carry me home
Swing low, sweet chariot
Coming for to carry me home

(*LARRY continues playing SWING LOW, SWEET CHARIOT*)

A Negro spiritual, the folk music of my own people. Again, the pentatonic scale! (*LARRY plays the introduction to ERISKAY LOVE LILT*) The five black keys of the piano! Here's another one.

(*Sings*)

Ver mee o O rovan O
Ver mee o O rovan Ee
Ver mee o ru oho
Sad am I without thee...

(*LARRY continues*)

That's called "An Eriskay Love Lilt," and that too is based on the pentatonic scale! And you know where it's from? The Hebridean Islands off the Coast of Scotland! (*Piano stops. PAUL getting more and more excited, and beginning to imagine more voices*) Go to Australasia, China, the Middle East, anywhere, it's the same thing. Music is a universal language based on the pentatonic scale. It's just that we hear it, we make it in different ways, like we speak different languages, and in different accents, see?

Now I, Paul Robeson, scholar/athlete, Paul Robeson, internationalist and musicologist, Paul Robeson, Negro – am going to write about it, talk about it, and sing it! To get the message across to the people of the world, that we are all brothers. ...The Mandarin Chinese say, "woaman dao shoar shung de" Yes sir! You bet I'm going to get the message across... about ...la fraternité du monde ...Mi vsyor braati! and... What? (*Behind him*) Who's there? Those darn voices! It's getting too much. I can't take it any more. I CAN'T TAKE IT ANY MORE! (*Sits in chair USC*) (*The sound of a crackling record and a crowd of people at a party are heard. Pianist starts to play discordant chaotic music*)

(*Beat*)

I'm at a party. So many people. Too many voices! Got to get out. (*Tries to get up, falls back*) They've drugged me! Got to get back home to Essie. But there's no escape. (*Rises*) I rush upstairs to the bathroom. My head feels like it's blowing up like a balloon! The voices are screaming at me now: "End it Paul, end it! Find peace. Find peace!" I try to open a window to jump out, to end it all, but my head's too big! I scramble in the cabinet – there must be some pills, a razor someplace? "End it Paul, end it. Find Peace, find..." Yes! A razor! There's no time to think. Just... (*Slits wrist*) Find peace, (*Slits other wrist*) find peace!" (*Sings*) I gets weary an sick of tryin' (*Stands, speaks*) Oh, that darn song! (*Sits, sings*)... I'm tired of livin' an scared of dyin'...

(*Pause*)

Ah, at last (*Piano music resolves to tuneful rendition of STEAL AWAY Reprise. A loud and gradually slowing heartbeat is heard*)... That feels better. I begin to float... Higher and higher... I see Essie and Pauli waving goodbye... Gerry Neale tells me that she loves me and wants to marry me after all. Yolande Jackson too. Oh, feels so good... I'm not sick any more... Not scared. Just – tired. So, so tired... I'll just go to sleep, and when I wake up... I'll be home... In the promised land, with Pop... with Mom...

(Slips out of consciousness. Piano plays last line of STEAL AWAY and stops. Heartbeats fade out. Pause. He wakes up with a start, and looks round, as if taking a moment to register where he is.)

I woke up, in the hospital, and as you can see, I lived to tell the tale. But I was sick for months. But Essie - and Helen, they looked after me. Pauli took me up to my sister Marian in Philadelphia. There was so much medication to take. I couldn't even read. Couldn't concentrate. The voices, see? I'd stay in my room, with the curtains drawn, day and night. Couldn't let them in, see? Didn't want anybody to see me that way. I just needed to rest, get my strength back. Then in the middle of all this, just when – *(He is interrupted by voice over)*

VOICE 1   CALL MR ROBESON!

PAUL   What?

VOICE 1   CALL MR ROBESON!!   The committee will be in order.

VOICE 2   This afternoon the committee resumes its series of hearings on the vital issue of the use of American passports as travel documents in furtherance of the objectives of the communist conspiracy. Defendant, please identify yourself by name, residence and occupation.

PAUL (*Appearing dazed, slow and uncomfortable*) My name is Paul Robeson. I live at 16 Jumel Terrace, New York City, and I am an actor and singer by profession, and law on the side, now and then.

VOICE 3   Are you appearing today in response to a subpoena which was served upon you by the House Committee on Un-American Activities?

PAUL   Yes sir, I am.

VOICE 4   Did you file a passport application on July 2nd, 1954?

PAUL Yes sir, I have filed several – about 25 in the last few months.

(*Coughs repeatedly, gets up and goes USR to the piano to take a tablet with some water, then addresses the audience*)

I had insisted on testifying, see? I thought I still had some fight left in me, but now I knew I was wrong. I said to myself, "Well, this is it, Robey, this is where you get crucified, and boy, did you ask for it this time". And then, all of a sudden this Negro woman comes into my mind. (*The sound of a Djembe is heard. PAUL moves slightly downstage in direction of vision*) She's got – her face is – it's my mother! No, no – this woman's even more beautiful. Ebony black. Her thick hair is sculpted in the shape of a Sankofa bird. Her eyes look straight into mine. Straight into my soul. Her face is wise. She knows everything. She's seen all there is to see, from the dawn of time. It's Mother Africa! Her spirit envelopes me, like I'm wrapped in a hibiscus-scented cloud, under the cool, cool shade of a celestial baobab tree, and I feel safe. Calm. She opens her mouth. Her voice is sweet. It flows out of her like from the bottom of a deep, deep river. She says to me, "Be strong, son. Be strong. I am with you. The ancestors are with you. Nwe Okukwe. Ujo Atunagi. (*Moving slowly backwards, back to chair*) Be strong. Be strong. Be strong..." and then she disappears. (*Sits. The sound of the interrogation continues over the Djembe*)

VOICE 4   Mr Robeson? (*PAUL refocuses*) ...Mr Robeson! Are you now a member of the Communist Party?

PAUL   As far as I know, it is a legal party like the Republican Party or the Democratic Party. It is a party of people who have sacrificed for my people and for all Americans and workers, that they may live in dignity.

VOICE 5   Have you ever been known under the name of John Thomas?

PAUL   Oh please! My name is Paul Robeson, and anything I have to say I have said in public all over the world, and that is why I am here today.

65

VOICE 3   Who is Manning Johnson?

PAUL   Manning Johnson... Oh, I read in the papers that he was dismissed from the FBI. He must be a pretty low character when he should be dismissed from that.

VOICE 4   Tell us whether or not you know Thomas W Young.

PAUL   I invoke the fifth amendment.

VOICE 4   Thomas W Young is the Negro publisher of The Journal and Guide. He took an oath before this committee, and testified as follows:

"Mr Robeson is now so far out of touch with Negro thinking, that he can no longer speak authoritatively about or for the race. In the eyes of the Negro people this false prophet is regarded as unfaithful to their country, and they should now repudiate him."

        Do you know the man who said that?

PAUL   I invoke the fifth amendment.

VOICE 3   Did you go to Moscow in 1949?

PAUL   Oh, yes. And I would say that in Russia I felt like a full human being for the first time in my life, and no colored prejudice like in Mississippi and no colored prejudice like I feel in the committee today.

VOICE 2   Why did you not stay in Russia?

PAUL   Because my father was a slave, and my people died to build this country, and I am going to stay here and have a part of it just like you. And no fascist minded people will drive me from it. Is that clear?

VOICE 4   While you were in Moscow, Mr Robeson, did you make a speech lauding Stalin?

PAUL   I will discuss Stalin when I may be among the Russian people some day, singing for them.

VOICE 4   Do you know Ben Davis?

PAUL   One of my dearest friends, one of the finest Americans you can imagine, and nothing can make me prouder than to know him.

VOICE 3   Did I understand you to laud his patriotism?

PAUL   I say that he is as patriotic an American as there can be, and you gentlemen belong with the Alien and Sedition Acts, and you are the non-patriots, and you are the un-Americans, and you should be ashamed of yourselves. And you are not fit to sit there questioning-

VOICE 1   (*Interrupts*) Just a minute. I have endured as much of this as I can. The hearing is now adjourned.

PAUL   I think it should be adjourned forever! (*Beat. Djembe sound fades*)

(*Pause*)

> The struggle continues. There are several more court hearings. Hopes raised, hopes dashed. It takes a lot out of me, but my friends and supporters, they all stand by me, they help me. And Pauli and Marilyn; my brother, Ben; my sister, Marian. And of course, Essie – she's with me all the time, like she'd always been. My rock!

(*Rises*)

> Eventually, one day in my brother Ben's church: The Mother Africa Methodist Episcopal Zion in Harlem.

(*LARRY plays along to the next sequence, improvising on OH, FREEDOM! in black gospel style*)

> Brothers and sisters, I have come to the end of a long, hard, road. Often times, when I could see no light, when I could see no end to my troubles, I would ask myself: What would my father say if he were alive today? He would say: "Oh yes! It is

hard, son, but don't forget that I was born in slavery and that your people were not able to do anything as free people for a long, long while. But they fought, they made their songs, they struggled ahead, and they escaped by the Underground. So, you stand your ground, son! You may have to stand there for a little while longer, you know. But just keep your courage and keep your heart." And that, brothers and sisters, is just what I did. And at long last, I am before you, and I testify that "Here I stand, and I got my passport in my hand!"

(With a huge grin, he holds up the passport for all to see. LARRY continues from OH, FREEDOM! into DIDN'T MY LORD DELIVER DANIEL, PAUL Sings)

Didn't my Lord deliver Daniel
Deliver Daniel, deliver Daniel
Didn't my Lord deliver Daniel
And why not-a every man
He delivered Daniel from the lions den
Jonah from the belly of de whale
An de Hebrew chillun from de fiery furnace
An' why not-a every man

(Piano stops)

I'm free to travel again, and I waste no time! I'm off to Europe with Essie. We do England, Wales, Scotland, Ireland, Russia. *(Piano plays opening*

69

notes of melody of GIT ON BOARD) Round and round! I sing! I speak! I play Othello! Everywhere, I feel nothing but – love!

(*Sings a cappella*)

> Git on board, little children
> Git on board, little children
> Git on board, little children

I can go anywhere I please! The Caribbean, East Germany, Australia, New Zealand. I'm away for five whole years, then back home to the US of A!

(*Sings, with piano accompaniment*)

> Git on board, little children
> Git on board, little children
> Git on board, little children
> There's room for many a more
>
> The gospel train's a coming
> I hear it just at hand
> I hear de car wheels rollin'
> An' rumblin' thru' de lan'
>
> Git on board, little children
> Git on board, little children
> Git on boa...

(*Stops suddenly. Pause*)

Essie died.

(*Sits in chair, CS*)

She'd had cancer, but never told me how bad it was. (*Pause. Piano starts playing introduction to JUST A WEARYIN' FOR YOU*) Once, years ago, when I told her how much I loved her — over the phone. She says to me, "What the hell are you talking about, Paul Robeson? Are you feeling alright?"

(*Chuckles and then almost breaks down. Sings, haltingly*)

Just A wearyin' for you
All the time A feelin' blue
Wishin' for you, wonderin' when
You'll be comin' home again.
Restless, don't know what to do
Just A wearyin' for you.

(*Piano continues under speech*)

Essie didn't really want to go back to America, you know. She preferred England, or Russia. But I was feeling restless. (*Rises. Goes to get medicine and water*) I felt I had been away too long, and needed to get back home, to take part in the continuing struggles of my people – now officially known as "The Civil Rights Movement." (*Piano stops. PAUL finds photo*)

Yes, I'd been hearing a lot about those new young fellows, like him. Malcolm X. Now, he'd been causing quite a stir; getting a lot of bad press, and being portrayed as advocating violence against whites. He'd broken with the Nation of Islam, travelled in Africa, and that changed him. He began to wonder if a brand of socialism might have something to offer the Black Man. Word came that he wanted to meet with me. I was so excited! The meeting was all set up, and then... they gunned him down. His own people, we'd be led to believe. But you know, I reckon the FBI were behind that. In the interests of National Security, of course.

(*Beat. Piano starts to play WE SHALL OVERCOME*)

About a year after I got back to America, I was approached by this young Negro reporter in Harlem. He was canvassing the opinion of "the Negro on the street" about the Montgomery Bus Boycotts, and he asked me what I thought. Well, I said that I fully supported Martin Luther King and his people, and that their action was proof that the Negro will not rest until he attains full equality and dignity. I said they were carrying on a great tradition of people who went before. Like

Frederick Douglass, like Ida Wells, Toussaint L'Ouverture, Harriet Tubman, Sojourner Truth, and so many others.

(*Beat*)

Well (*incidental music stops abruptly*) ...King was shot dead too. Buried on my 70th birthday as it happens. And he was only 39. Then, the CIA. They helped kill Patrice Lumumba in the Congo... And you watch: Walter Sisulu and Nelson Mandela, they'll probably die in jail too.

(*Beat*)

Now, that young reporter. He asked me who he could quote. (*Beat. Surprised*) Paul Robeson, I said. Paul... Robeson? No, no. R - o - b - E - s - o - n. (*Beat*) He thanks me, shakes my hand, and then walks right on to the next person! (*Shakes his head, incredulous*) Seems I'd been assassinated too! Not sure when exactly.

(*Beat*)

So, with Essie gone, what's the point of carrying on? Why don't I just end it all? (*Sits SC*) I thought about it, but then I decided, "Well, there's still Pauli, there's his wife, Marilyn, there's the grandchildren, and then there's my public, both in

America and all over the world. I can't go that way."

(Beat. Remembers something, then goes to pick up photo of W E B Du Bois)

My great friend and mentor, Dr W E B Du Bois: he chose to end his days in Africa (*The sound of a Djembe is heard*) – in Ghana. He'd always reminded us Negroes that Africa was our home, that we should hold our heads high, and not let slavery make us forget the proud histories and achievements of our ancestors. He suggested that maybe I should go to Nigeria, where I believe my people were stolen from. A little late for that now, I fear, but I have no regrets. Africa is home, alright. I've always known that, but I don't need to be there to feel it. It's always been (*taps his chest*) here. Always will be. (*Replaces photo. Djembe stops. Beat*) Well, (*Piano starts to play opening chords to GOIN' HOME*) the freedom train has taken my people that much closer to our destination now, and I tried to do my share of the driving. When the time's right – but not before – I'll get off at my stop, and slip right on home.

(The sound of an African rattle)

(Sings)

74

Goin' home, goin' home
I'm a-goin' home
Quiet like some still day
I'm just goin' home...

It's not far, jes' close by
Through an open door
Work all done, care laid by
Gwine to fear no more....
Mother's there 'spectin' me
Father's waitin' too
Lots o' folk gathered there...
All the friends I knew,
All the friends I knew.

(*The sound of a crackling vinyl record returns. Piano continues quietly underneath as he speaks*)

"Soft you, a word or two before you go.
I have done the state some service, and they know't.
No more of that. I pray you, in your letters,
When you shall these unlucky deeds relate,
Speak of me as I am. Nothing extenuate,
Nor set down aught in malice."

(*Sings*)

Home... Home...
I'm goin'...

(Piano pauses as he picks up the chair. Rejoins him as he carries on singing and heads for exit USL)

Home!

(As he reaches exit, lights fade to black)

END OF PLAY